CW01637758

LIFE LINES

SIMON MACK

This edition first published in paperback by
Michael Terence Publishing in 2023
www.mtp.agency

ISBN 9781800946989

Cover image
Simon Mack

Cover design
Copyright © 2023 Michael Terence Publishing

Michael Terence
Publishing

Acknowledgements

I'd like to pay my respects to the acquaintances, strangers, scenarios and situations that have inspired the works within.

Thank you to the 'raw' for their assistance with this collage of angles.

Introduction

Within these pages you will find a series of creative works that were inspired by a moment.

Standing solitary in the arrivals hall of being, the experiences that wander by arouse occasional urges to paint feelings or observances with words.

These works form an erratic written artwork of those experiences that motivated creation.

They do not formulate into judgement or reason, and their genesis and ultimate theme belongs with the reader to interpret in their own manner.

I very much hope that you enjoy your journey through 'Life Lines', and if this book achieves anything at all it is a memoir to 'We are not alone in our thoughts, weaknesses and adventures.'

Contents

Empathy

An empathy with sorrow
With loss
With erosion
With pain
With defeat
With the battle
With the fear
With your torment
With consequence
With shame
With anger
With what was
With what will be.

Self-gratification
A grotesque beast
The first and the only
No passengers
No dead weight
Yet we are the levy
A tariff unwanted
Disrespected
Disregarded.

Mainstream's involuntary outcasts
Spirits stripped of abandon
Beleaguered souls
Grimacing smiles into the cold painful night
As they pass…
Without a glance
They notice but choose ignorance
Consciousness a nuisance of a side show
A side street dalliance wasting time.

So to the rush…
Whilst we hobble
We roll
We crawl
We lay
Together in stoic determination
Not to give up.

A shrine to the perseverance of dreams
Beacons of differing triumph
Solitary lights
Together illuminating the insanity about
They may choose to not see us
But we see them
Without prejudice
For we have the scars
Etched with scale
Beyond the flow
Only warm.

Us

The merging of the blood
In war
In love
By accident and choice
A vial of vile
A flask of hope
A beaker of joy
A decanter of hate
All pouring into an ocean of bodily fluids named truth
Our reality
Our evil
Our compassion
Our depravity
Our care
Our filth
Cascading together
Secrets blending with outrage
Devotions intertwining deceit
We are all
Every elation and all despondency on our hands
Open palms bathed with a claret lather of consequence
Clotting culminations of our deploy
The door maybe closed and the window bolted
But it will ooze

Seeping...
Meandering in shameful pride into the sea of us
For whatever we deny and despise it all goes on
Because it is all us
No matter what faith
Irrelevant race
Political persuasion or denomination
It's all IN here
Eclectically merged
Irrevocably combining
Bigoted views won't matter once you reach our shore
Witness our modes
Accept our deeds
Concede a collective genesis
Comprehend our darkness
Absorb our gentleness.

This is no religion
No cult
No sect
You won't have to pay
Be abused or hurt
Because all that's been done is in here already
To understand is to accept
To accept is to commence.

Humdrum End

The broken pieces
Infinite shards
The pane of my life
A puzzle beyond resolution
How was this the result?

The avenues of being
Driven in a vehicle bereft of direction
Am I at fault for this lack of destination?
This void of destiny
This lack of comprehension
Just what should I do?
What should I be?
How can I achieve?
Each turning of opportunity dashed by the sinews of self-doubt
Just a little way along hard on the brakes
A hasty reversal to the leafy avenues of humdrum
My how monotonous

Until the smash
My broken pieces drifting about the tarmac of resignation
Delivered to a destination signposted regret
Pressed into the ground by the wheels of emboldened brash
Souls embracing opportunity
Crushing me into oblivion
Irrelevance's eradication
The end of humdrum.

Sands

Grabbing at sand
Stretched hands gulping
Billowing loss between fingers
Beyond palms
A decree of impossible dimension
I have failed.

Plunging again with cup of digits
Modest loads blown
Adrift on the breezes of time
Each scoop absconds
Falling back
Just as before.

Lifting and failing
Sifting through claw like formations
Perpetual returns
No sign of a spade
No mechanical aid
A task of futile demands
Acceptance's mandate.

For the hair will fall too through whisps of time
The wrinkles multiply
Aches worsen
A late-night payback days into debt
Staring at the sands
Billowing away.

As idols pass
Loved ones expire
A generation's turn draws closer
Greed fuelled snatches at the floors of time as useless as the growing prose in this verse
Our reckoning draws ever closer
As those we held dear fall to the gritty whisps of fate
Acceptance is all.

Escape Illusion

The wonder of evasion
A joy in immersion
Detour from grind's expectation
Assuming our effort
Consuming our will
Swept under a carpet woven escapism
Of these moments no despair
Tidied into a box for another fight
Ailments and pains on pause
Waiting outside a bolted door
For now there is peace in solace's regeneration
The blocks repaired
A sub conscious remedy without explanation
Missing deadlines in carefree commute
I am at large… just for now.

I won't abuse myself or others
No comfort in corruption
The courting of contortion another's tipple
Riding elusively just for a while
Immersed
Familiar
Unbothered
Liberated
At peace
Home.

Our lives a disease
Enacted for millennia
Minds & souls owned by others
Spirit for hire to pay whom?
Fund what?
Prisons we created
Cages inhabited freely for what gain?
Today's incarceration subtle
Drip fed
A hazy mix of mind tricks and perception
All the same… captives with permitted brief abscond.

I'll use licensed abandon carefully
And ensure as the door locks behind me I have enough breath
Renewed strength and the will to get through my sentence
The term is long escape's fortunes slight
May fleeting brightness linger long enough to cleanse my hatred of this circle
Fortitude's grace come gently
Before the contorted gurn of demand is dribbling the saliva of greed upon me once more
In this moment a sanity.

Flash the Trash

What's with the constant devaluation?
Is decency a worthless trait?
Is dignity no longer of stock?
Are graces now an irrelevance unfathomable?
But then it dawned
The value of allure in all its brazen obvious ungraciousness
is now key to society's notice
No room for ambiguity
It's just… there… for all to gaze
And you don't need to be present to witness.

An ultimate motive to spray unbridled visage to every
corner
Because that garners views
Likes
Shares
Follows
Comments
Contact
Lust
Play
Want
Yet only objectively
Selfishly
Callously
Lustfully
They'll consume your display only for self-gratification
Because that's what got delivered

A neat bow topped full frontal exposure of a piece of flesh
For others to digest in bar or social platform in drooling wanton anarchy
And when the results are delivered will we cry foul?
As a matador prodding the arse of a raging bull with a hot poker
Should he be shocked when the beast gores his guts through?

Suggestion, disgust and foul deeds likely subsequent bedfellows
A raging horned monster not your intention yet you stood mid ring wearing bright red anyway.

What has been created?
A realm where all is on display
An audacious skimpy fuck you or just conformity to the tide?
A necessity to be of the crowd marked of modern relevance?
Compliance of flow without conscious note?
It won't matter
Because the line will be crossed
And when it is time for blame it will be of contention
Deplore for deeds unlawful served of wilful opportunity
What was wrong with the days of grace?
Of panache

Of manners
Of Mystique
A time when innocence and respect where preserved and respected
Not hung out to dry with last night's booze-stained thong
A person's dignity was of asset
Aspirational even
Valued
Preserved
Respected
Time has changed boundaries but the foundations of life's weakness prevail
Sexism
Racism
Defame
Power
Cruelty
Spite
Jealousy
All diseases erected by humanity
Weak to the whims of their own demons
Their scars broadcast upon you because the door was open to do so
Some say "Their problem."
Don't let it become yours too
Life was never as innocent as it seemed
Publicly boundaries and values decided

Is it time to put them back?
Depravity away from young influenced & aspirational eyes?
Rebuild society's interaction
Foundations of mannerly respect
Rather than use and dispose?

Borrowers

Borrowers
A dynasty of rentals
What is ownership?
Whose deeds are they?
Materialistic irrelevance
Custody's aspiration
Departed with a waft of fate.

To the soil
Uncontrollable breezes of dust
A notion's disintegration
Gusting away
Sweat no more
Consumptions passing
And behind us?
Heaps of irrelevance?

The needs and the wants
Distorted by publication
Force fed
Mind infected
To take
To spend
To squander
To amass
To fritter
Surrounded by things
Objects of desire
Delivering nothing.

Impaired planet
Inhabitants misplaced
Incarcerated by depravity
Requisite's presumption
Disinterest fundamental
Ecology's woe
The plastics of the sea dancing in a tide of the blind
We court beauty yet destroy it all
To the fire.

Bitter Lemons

The altar of my past
Growing ever taller than before
A monument to regret
Epitaph to choice of wrong direction
The sands of history wafting below
Wisping about on the breeze of ignorance
A gritty squint through stone lashed storm baptised
'opportunity'
Styled of 'confidence'
Dubbed 'seizure'
Concocted incomprehension
A honed 'glimpse'
A chaffed gaze straight at squander
Sacred edifice of hindsight
Flailing arms gesticulated repent
Exasperated rear view
Knees amidst dune
A wealth of chances shatter
Compliant to the ground through paralysed digits
A fixed gaze in remorse
A box set of recollections entitled 'What if?'
Living mistakes
Bitter lemons.

LA BUERLIN

Space

I'll buy the house at the end of the village
The last on the row
With a gap to the rest
Close enough to interact
Far enough away to distance
I like the peace
The segregation
The effort to visit a favourable barrier
Unless invited
(Which happens rarely)
A jaunt away
I can't hear their weakness
No infection of expectation
A clear path lays between
And here alone I can mine admission
Removing the legs of those I abhor
Splattering the genitals of irritation onto a pavement of disregard
A deepening solitude
Mental challenges created by me
I cannot amend
This is who I am
Detachment's cramp?
Attachment's stitch?

For me no choice
Solitude is not of option but rather of comfort
A recluse for equilibrium
Please remain your side of the fence
Trespassing unsettles
And awkward ensues.

Assortment

An assortment of people
A disparate spread
The showy divorcee
The considered man
The elderly couple
The boys on the piss
The frantic messenger
The knowing smile
The nervous aggression
The accounting looks
Assessors
Table cleaners
A cafe of souls at differing angles
Together of kindred choice
Tall and loving
Stumpy and grumpy
Cry to sly
Flicking looks
Inquisitive
Suspicious
Wanting
Unable to admit desires
Prohibited by the protocol of human decorum
Silence
Boundary

The wanders of want
Consulted to a halt
Too much toil for the wilds
A dice afflicted with pain
Ache's yearning
Temptations sting
Calm's implore
Occurring's ensemble
Will anyone break perceived civility?
Does chaos follow?
A jumble of the mind
Amongst this Melé of constraint
To the toilets…?

The Barrage

The onslaught's obtuse devastation
Consistent despair
Frequent longing
Constant fear.

A barrage bereft of sanity
Conducted by pawns
Misinformed tyrannical disciples
Equally intimidated.

Decisive tendencies
Way above Tom, Dick & Harriet
Whatever your preference
Games beyond outstretched grasp.

Political ping pong
Corporate cowardice
Whoever's blame or crime
We will all pay.

With solitary solution
Our toxic dilemma
Mass action our option
Scepticism the retort.

Conceived of mild ambition
Now ruling the world
Misinformation at all juncture
Shattering consensus.

We are all fucked
Yet we wired our fate
Our ancestors dreams
We inhabit as a nightmare.

Pass

And as they pass we stay behind in fields travelled by loss
Footsteps to the distance
Rutted with memories
Sewed in our woe
We endure the green shoots of pain…
Standing Sober
Furrowed brows of decline
As they walk away to the horizon never to return.

The lamenting rains came
Splashing our faces as we grimace inti a cold dank woe
A creased brow of penance
For they go those we love
Not to speak
Not to repair ever again
For all that went before is now stone
Carved of mouth and deed
Never to be taken back
Epilogues completion
Covers closed.

And what for those that remain to experience the march?
Awaiting their beckon
Will we grasp our time to rewrite the grotesque?
To convey concession
To display compassion
Before we are called and deeds become granite
Will we chisel the mountain?
Correcting its ridges
Leaving a sculpture of lesser distaste
Do they care anyway those who stand and watch our final paces?
To stand harder than to walk
Feet fastened in regret
The watery eyes of loss
This is life
Ageing envoys
To be bitter or to glow as we are called?
Choices of the living days recalled
Disappearing blips on a horizon of no amend
Editors in life of monoliths to decision now beyond gaze.

Its Time

The days of rabid consumption are over
Turn off the lights as you leave
Wade wake's path to reach the gas guzzler
A drive thru burger with sachet of ignorance's relish
Take a ride to the hairpin signposted responsibility
Any sight of the bend?
No… just a blinkered plough… straight through the fields of flouting
Smashing through the fences of gestures and conferences
Self-gratifying choice to just not bother
Allied with a social feed not accepting flow of factual inconvenience
Someone else's challenge.

A leader's strife
A neighbours concern
A child's fear
Devastating futures in the face of aspiration
A hedonistic broken system of perpetual need
"One day"
One dawning day of priorities reckoning
But when is that morning?
How will it become?
When your own personal island of chosen ignorance becomes a physical reality?
When you boat the kids to school as the Chelsea tractor sinks to a watery grave?

Take a turn…
The curve to the mutual responsibility of the future we leave
And when it's time for us to depart and hand on the baton
afford the hand of hope the ability to grasp our legacy
Brushing aside the palm of despair
Will you continue to gather with the architects of the end?
Set aside our devouring self-centred ambitions?
Open the gates to the possibility of a tomorrow?
For humanity thereafter
And those born of this very day
Your… OUR new direction
A sat nav heading marked "collective change"
We are tomorrow.

Grains

The days came the went
Ever changing skies
Through window's static gaze
All seasons passed in springs unpredictable hues
I never moved
Branches swayed waving over glistening rooftops
Moist of winters shower
Tufts of moss collect sustenance within the crevices
Enthralled by gravity
Antennas jostle to the tune of the wind
Telephone wires wrestle with the taught suspension of A to B
Repetitive flash denotes alarms warning not to try it
Especially not at the minute
Tightly packed dwellings laced with ailment
A time upon to bear the brunt
As we'd hidden before now we sit with legs crossed and eyes closed
The coming storm audible
Predictable
Known
Our secluded avoidance no longer an option
They come like the mists of an air born desert's grain
To engulf us
Infect us

We will breath
Me must inhale
And as we did becoming unwanted hosts to the inevitable
To the window's view
The wait
The battle
For all that we tried
All we sacrificed
These days symptoms of our time
A result of humanity's tinker
Our superiority checked
A truth upon us
Self-imposed blazed destruction a pathway into scorched future
With loss and weakened brow we will face it
A bitter medicinal lesson
Our throne denied.

Cyber Sloth

Lived from my stinking bed
Defecating here as the sheets stained and matted
Remnants about of the greasy sustenance a chap in a beaten car had hurled through my window
"Where's the ketchup you asshole!?"
He didn't care
I didn't tip
Fuck em
With my splendid promenade of digital devices I did shop
Gaze
Nose
Study
Waste
Ply
Maintain
Titivate and toil
The bounds of my mind the only prohibition
No need or desire to move
And soon my room stank
Thick with the scent of lax
My waistline rapidly expanding allied with nonchalant depravity
But I didn't care

There was no whim that couldn't be serviced as I grew
hairy
As any good 21st century societal wookiee like hermit
prick would
"Why do they phone me?"
Actual human interaction an unnecessary dalliance
Yes I might now resemble something from a medieval
slurry trench but the birds on here are tidy!
A full 4K HD wide screen stream of those who do bother
to preen
But no need for me
I'll dwell within a cyber sloth paradise.

Twisted

The memory twists
Morphing reality into a convenient tale
Of bias
Of angle
Of convenience
Of political motive
Of bullshit
Of enchantment
Sometimes encouraged
Often spread
A gnarly puss weeping boil on the arse of reality
Wobbling it's way around all gullible or nosey enough to squeeze
Morphing the sore beyond ugliness
Until the beast foretold is of unspeakable disgust and depravity
How did we get here?
What is this 'thing'?
Unrecognisable
A disgraceful spoken turd of utter nonsense
Caressed by those with jealous, selfish or bitchy motive
Cultivated by those full of void and boredom
Do I care?
Does it hurt?
Yes it does… sometimes

Will it ruin my life?
No
Do I seek revenge?
Vindictiveness against stupid is futile
What will you do?
Ignore it and them
They can all look then piss off
Truth may lie within
But they couldn't care less!
For the falsehood fireworks of slander are more fun
And in my suffering twisted pleasure.

Freeing

We won't be hard to find
Rutted in decision
Railed to a system
Invested in pattern
Undeterred by option
The same
We like the same
Settled on routine
Uncharted choices never in favour
Its written
Regular
Familiar
Trodden
Lines
We like grids
Riddled with cards we can always predict
It makes us happy
We are orderly
So be gone to the wilds
Leave us here
We prefer the known that is our liberation.

Cobra

The cobra came in the night
Raised
Wide
Spitting filth
Writhing
Contorting
Swirling with fury
Aroused
Intention attack
Terrorise
Dismantle
Erode
Petrify.

My mind swirls
Recoiling
Uncontrollable paranoia
A sprit's desolation
Confidence's waste
A happiness drained
To the sewer of despair
No rest
No peace
No calm

For the asp remains
Throwing forward in paralysing jousts
Relentless
Curling around my hope
Squeezing until extinct.

There will be no tranquillity
There can't be a future
Merely the quiver of now in anguished perpetuity.

Inglorious Mess

The difficult essence
I am of it
Like most of the rest
Turbulent little shit.

Conformity's pressure
Decrees of others
Bearing down upon you as a petulant unwanted bastard
A turd perched on your nose
Stinking
Decaying
An unwanted hair in the soup of my recipe
Pestering
Nagging
Unyielding in pressure
Spraying an unwelcome shower of forceful diarrhoea directly into my miserable kisser
Yet that face must smile as the faeces drip onto a shirt of despair
And those feet must dance on the soiled floor of demand
I am an arduous fuck because I just don't want to
Can't be bothered
Do not like
Gain no enjoyment
Feel awkward
And to subject to the above there must be faith

Belief
Compassion
Comprehension and care
Not just expectation and decree
I comprehend my shit is another's chocolate
And whilst the colour and texture can bear similarities
synergy requires a floating snickers
For I'd rather not become engulfed in the waste matter of your expectations
And you'd prefer to guzzle from the base of the confectionery fountain for eternity
A breach in discord of king-size Twix proportion
A mixture of both a creation of a repulsive demeanour..
Yes shit and chocolate must cohabit
In aggravated perpetuity
Pebble dashing the walls with grievance
Is the poop valid in its spread?
Is the galaxy of sweet treats righteous in its existence?
Will there be deification onto the confectionery?
A plethora of brown
Seemingly of no formula appropriate
A "choco" shit party ensues
Oh what an inglorious mess.

Frauds

They seemed so smiley and nice
In truth they were cunts
A paper thin facade
Upturned mouth heading south…
Faster than a toupee in a hurricane
If you thrash out their tune the veil will remain
If you choose a genre distasteful down comes the cloth
Revealing a wretched reality
Like dynamite mining in a quarry..
Behind the curtain a shattered splintered face
Pleasantries over
Manner's Cease
What an ugly truth
Like the hairy shitty arse of an incontinent pensioner
Weeping faeces in wild abandon
Stained
Foul
Wretchedly real
The gravity of past falsehoods unfathomable
Who are these vile scrotes?
And how on earth can I get rid of their rancid effigies?
Fuck off you frauds!

Selfie

The selfie
More like self-centred?
An instant's grin
The furrowed remainder
For all the momentary images of sun surrounded by storms
The clouds of realism
The breaks manufactured
Scribbling a falsehood of impossible aspiration
Untruths splatted everywhere anyone may gawp
The images idyll factuality drenched on shores emblazoned with despair
Does the facade enrich?
Do the expectations generated nourish?
Is this piece just a sycophantic pastiche veiled in envy?
Or would I rather sandpaper my personal parts than coat myself with a faked veneer?
Each to their own but…
Unattainable falsehoods become the unachievable aspirations of others
Your fake
Their depression
An endless sphere smeared of social bullshit
Will they stand back to grasp?
Or slip down the a shitty slope signposted failure?

Their catastrophe
Foul life
Hateful job
Busted car
Scabby flat
So where the fuck are the photos coming from?
This cesspit town?
Throwaway fast food dinners & masturbation
Fleeting joys until they scroll
Fuck my life.

Sell Out Signs

Let's party…
No ta
Good vibes…
Oh dear
Dream big…
Please no
Sweet dreams…
You what?
The architects of nothing
Honed and refined on signage sold for £3.99 in stores filled with pointless
The unwanted
The ill though out
Havens of a mindless void
Inhabited by the 'Cocktails and Dreams' of cunts in delirium over a new burger at McDoodaa
"Oh wow two chicken burgers in one bun"
Whoopie.

Does it sound pretentious?
A purveyor of opinion perceived to look down or belittle?
Suggestions of expecting more
Thinking deeper
Stretch the horizon of mind's eye?
A disease collectively infected upon
Minor made tat from far away allied with a greasy sloth of a western consumption culture

It invaded your life and you didn't resist
As the high street of independence waved a collective white flag with no arms to battle
Tax dodging conglomerates
Slave labour manufacturing
Allied together in a perfect storm so you can abandon your local heritage and consume cheap meaningless junk
On your walls and down your gob
And just like the runny shit that frozen menagerie you bought from the drive thru created those who toil to supply your lazed demands will let out a yelp of despair as the consequences of our apathy and unscrupulous greed decree the toilet paper of life is wiped upon their face
Laden with the stains of our collective ignorance
This is freedom?

Rancid Mastication

Blinded ascent
Driven
Recklessly rising to perilous altitude
An incomprehensible ego driven climb
No reverse
Arrogant hurtle to inevitable nosedive.

As the clingers uncouple ignorance's expansion
Doors shut
Icy stares
No longer 'en vogue'
A walking repellent
Will your vanity amend?
Does your arrogance allow?
An unwelcome reality etched purposely
Crisis of your genesis
It all got too big
Status overload
Identity steroidal
Breaking down like the cheap grease laden kebab of demise your life has become
Nasty frozen tasteless oozing flesh
Filthy lettuce
Stinking onions
Mouldy pitas
Sour mayonnaise
You chomp… you wretch
Gagging in the face of your own arrogance

Suitors no longer suffer
Purpose expired
Number erased
Contact ignored
As you gawp at a deficient future
The wind of disfavour engulfs your rancid feast with the dusts of irrelevance
Keep chewing.

Stupid

Where is home?
Where is grace?
Where is dignity?
What is a peaceful place?

Call it rude
Call it front
Call it brash
Say it's a disgrace.

Tell them calm
Tell them kind
Tell them respect
Implore them to disregard.

Come to chaos
Come to void
Come to conclusion
Evade to retain sanity.

Drive to help
Drive to work
Drive to avoid
Sail to serenity beyond lost hope.

As the breeze through autumn leaves the noise of others is lost to the wind
Eradicated over a fence of pointlessness
From mouths around
Discrimination
Ignorance
Judgement
Of consequence only in your deeds
A tennis match empowered by knives
A refusal to play an understandable retort
Warring with stupid a fruitless attrition.

Balcony Despair

Unqualified bastards
Without a rudder
Bereft of tools to get by in life
Missing an engine
Lacking desire
Bankrupt in hope
Reliance on others
Independence null
Effort little
Self afflicted oblivion without comprehension
All others fault
A sect of victims incapable of confession
Ineptitude's epitome
A new mass state of uncultured sloths
Hypnotised by screens filled with splendour
Paralysed in idyllic unambitious hovels
To clean
To work
To aspire
To effort
To endure
To strive
To achieve
All utterly beyond the bounds of this unprincipled herd
Hypnotised by humdrum acquisition.

The sly just slip on by
The greedy exploit
The evil deploy
Yet this multitude of cursory humanity far too occupied to notice
With phones or shoes?
Woe abound
As elementary mind tricks bamboozle a cacophony of exploitable fools
Satisfied with the rancid scraps thrown down from a feasting table populated by the bulbous rotten greedy pompous arrogant walkers on high
The unqualified bastards and the greedy wankers
They are most welcome to each other
Neither the table or the floor enchant at all
To the chair… on the balcony named despair
We'll watch the game together
And witness this world flush slowly around a u-bend to the sewers of ruination
No escape from the flow & maybe ignorance preferable
Conscious catastrophe
A voluntary devourment of our mutual respect
Our integrity
Our future.

Junctures

Junctures
Moments
Judgements
Feelings
Shackles
Weights
Duties
Commitments
Fear
Tainted
Stained
Resistant.

Future's knock
A rap at the door marked chance
Pamphlet of opportunity wafting groundward
Letterbox of decision swinging in the winds of risk
Pendulum
Upon an aroma of the unfamiliar
Roads morph newly laid
Hazardous lane
Rapid progress?
Opaque horizons squint but glasses won't help
No clarity in commitments request
My decree required amidst the norm about
Safe
A known routine

Hawaiian shirts or string vests?
Contemplation brief
Splattering of all that has been and could be
And now to the hand
To grasp or deny?
Our palms glance as connection fades
For I am bound
Stained blouse of reprise taut
Seal up the opening
Call off the rollers
For there will be no aroma of fresh tarmac today
Trapped in a net sewn with my own needle of pathetic self-inflicted tangle
Here I'll remain
Interned with a bed fellow nicknamed misery
Let me scowl
Be gone.

Social Unsocial

If it's useless and inconsequential
Its videoed and posted
Toilet mirror selfie snaps
Captured and shared
Jacket potato lunch smeared with topping akin to dog faeces
Documented consumed and tagged
Ungracious cunt parked over a car park line
Publicly humiliated via social media group
And will you blur out their registration plate?
Will you fuck
"I had to walk another 10 paces because of that turd!"
But don't stress!
Some equally in gracious uncaring grunt will come up with their name in the comments.

Is this our society?
Is everyone else a nuisance or imposition?
Devoid of compassion
Bereft of humility
To be used for your own self-centred damaging gain?
Good grace erased
You won't yield
You won't stop
No time to think because it's all an orgy of self-gratification

I've seen my feed
I've witnessed the 'sunshine'
A social feast jam packed with scantily clad devourment
Gobble it all up
Build on an unattainable toilet roll long list of the fake
For that is NOT reality
That is not balance
That is impossible
A feed of sunshine bias bereft of the shade
The hues that make up life spun into a frenzy in warped grin
Attainment by wrongdoing considered
Desperation to realise without boundary
Yet all existence bites and all life wanders into the dark
The depths never posted unless for attention
Stings without post
All of life in a social turmoil
Skipping inconvenient truths
Until your eyes are permanently transfixed to the screen
Look up
You have become social unsocial.

Devoid

Don't speak it
Can't say that
Double check
Triple think
Zip it
Button up
Shhhhhhh
A woken box without flaps
Don't bulge
Never split
No pokes
Devoid of tears
Keep it sealed
Tensioned against penetration
Carted with both hands
Gripping relentlessly in fear of the 'drop'
For on impact splits
Pouring out truths in the face of la la la la la
For they don't want to hear the inconvenient
Better to blah blah blah
The game of bullshit devoid of fact
Allergic to compassion
Ignorant to sense

A perpetual bilge of manipulative output
A visage with only a mouth
Eyes and ears gouged and clogged with conveniences knife
Choose your words selectively
Or bark against the locked door of sanity
The world is void.

Shoot

Never give up dreaming
Despite a pain that extracts balance
Don't be denied
Obstruct prohibition
Expand into the chimney breast qualifying elaboration
Because you have the scope
The talent
The perception
The gift
And the ability to smash through the bollocks
Dismantle the mundane
Void a grind of interfering humdrum
Crush the ball bearings in the treadmill
Salute the hamster cage with a single raised finger
Deploy your skill
Back yourself
Swerve the tractor beam of monotony
As a ping pong ball fired from the mouth of a wannabee influencer in a video with no views
Shoot your stringy saliva every place you can
And infect all with an understanding of you
Because you have it
And they want a slice.

Epilogue

Once it has been said.

After effort's input, and observances have carved feeling; Scars are left over the damage endured on a mind that was once open to life's possibilities.

Yet whilst being affected both physically and mentally by interaction is unavoidable, the observances within these pages are not intended to be only of an empty glass.

Aspects of life through the ages can be bereft of learnings from humanity gone by, but our species inability to improve itself I do not allow to overshadow the brilliance, culture, kindness and toil for better that remains abundant in our world.

Whilst we all carry our burdens there remains pockets of bright light & blind despair, even if only for a little while.

Excuses are convenient, and criticism easier than the actions toward a more positive thereafter.

People have campaigned in the name of change for millennia, yet to enact change first there must be a conscious awakening to the need.

Collectively it's much simpler to bob along in the flow, and this angled prod at the current is a means to vent alert to the navigators of our species.

Be it deities or an ideology that assists your narrows, let light between the slats of the blinds… For a better tomorrow.

Available worldwide from Amazon

Michael Terence Publishing

www.mtp.agency

mtp.agency

@mtp_agency

Printed in Great Britain
by Amazon

36667805R00046